THE MOON

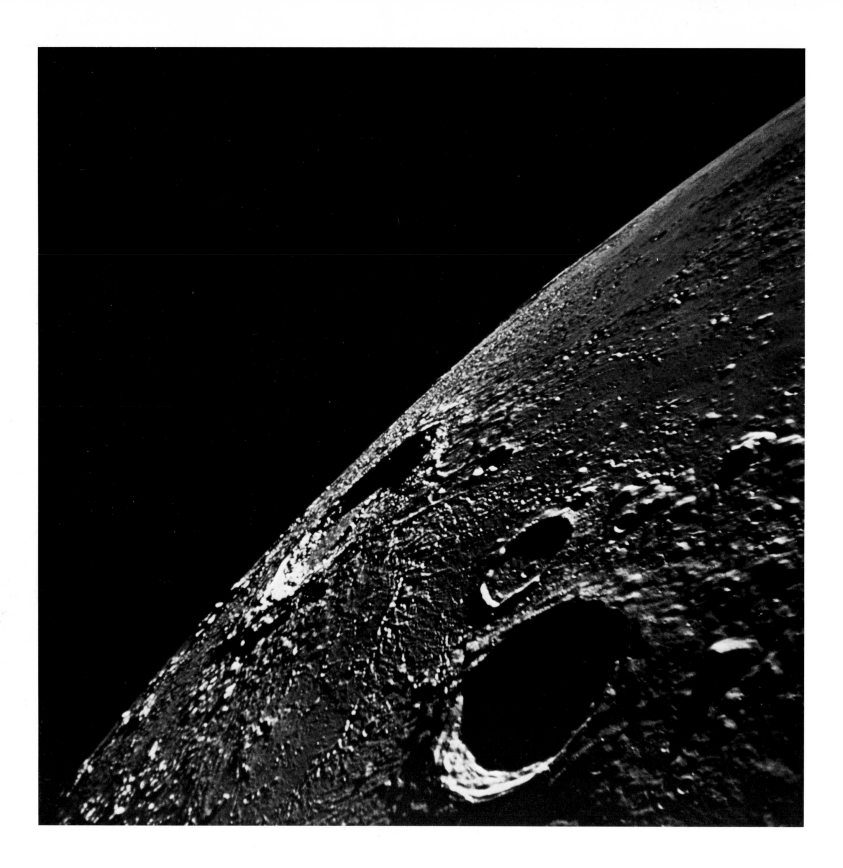

THE MOON

SEYMOUR SIMON

FOUR WINDS PRESS
NEW YORK

PICTURE CREDITS
The author wishes to acknowledge for the use of photographs:
NASA: Frontispiece, 7, 13, 14, 15, 16, 17, 18, 20, 21, 23, 24, 25, 26, 27, 29, 30, 32
Hale Observatories: 9
Mount Wilson and Palomar Observatories: 10, 11

10 9 8 7 6 5 4 3 2 1

The text of this book is set in 18 pt. Garamond.
The illustrations are black-and-white photographs.

Library of Congress Cataloging in Publication Data
Simon, Seymour.
The Moon.
Summary: A basic introduction to Earth's closest
neighbor, its composition, and man's missions to it.
1. Moon—Juvenile literature. 2. Moon—Photographs
from space—Juvenile literature. [1. Moon] I. Title.
QB582.S545   1984   559.9'1   83-11707
ISBN 0-590-07883-6

Remembering Irving Orlofsky

The moon is Earth's closest neighbor in space. It is about one quarter of a million miles away. In space that is very close.

The moon travels around Earth. It is Earth's only natural satellite. A satellite is an object that travels around another object. The moon takes about twenty-seven days and eight hours to go around Earth once.

The moon is so close to Earth that you can easily see light and dark places on its surface. This photograph of the moon was taken through a telescope on Earth. The light places are mostly mountains and hills. The dark places are flat lands.

The moon has thousands of craters covering its surface. Craters are ring-shaped flat lands with walls around them. The large crater at the bottom left of the photo is called Copernicus, after a famous astronomer. Copernicus is fifty miles wide. Some of the moon's craters are even larger but most are smaller. Many of the craters are only a few feet wide.

The moon is made of rock. We can see only the part of the moon lit by sunlight. Sometimes we see the full moon. Other times we see a thin sliver. Every night the moon looks a little different. Each different shape is called a phase of the moon. The phases go from an all-dark new moon through full moon and back to new moon in about twenty-nine days. We call the phase in the photograph a crescent moon.

From earliest times, people gazed up at the moon and wondered about it. Was the moon a world like ours? Were there living things on the moon? Would we ever be able to travel to the moon?

Over the years, scientists learned much about the moon by studying it from Earth with telescopes and other instruments. But many things were still unknown. Then in 1961, the United States Government decided to try to send a person to the moon within ten years.

The space program was named Apollo. This photo shows the Apollo 10 spaceship sixty miles above the moon's surface. It is flying over the far side of the moon, which we can never see from Earth.

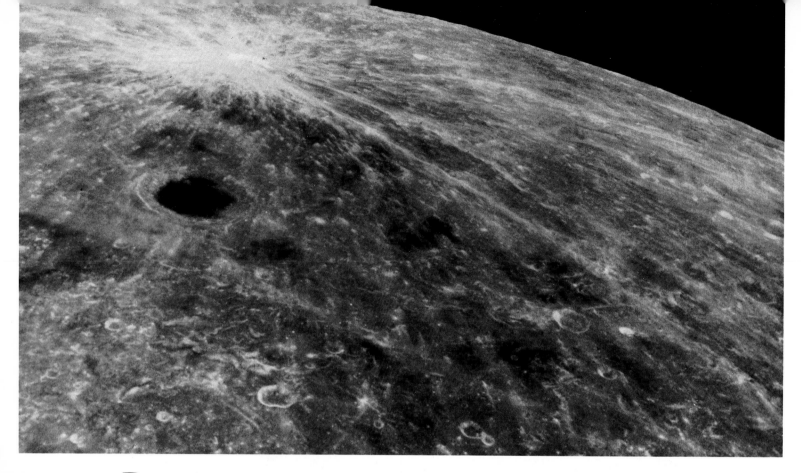

Before the space age, no one had ever seen the far side of the moon. That's because the same side of the moon always faces Earth. Then, spaceships from Earth went around the moon. Here is one of the photographs taken from a spaceship. It shows part of the moon's far side. You can see craters and mountains, much like those on the side of the moon we see from Earth. But the far side has few flat lands, or "seas."

On July 20, 1969, Neil Armstrong became the first person to set foot on the moon. Armstrong was one of the astronauts on the Apollo 11 flight to the moon. He was shortly followed by Edwin Aldrin, another member of the United States Apollo 11 space flight. This is a photograph of Astronaut Aldrin standing on the moon. The face mask of his space suit reflects Astronaut Armstrong.

This footprint on the moon marks the first time that human beings have walked on ground that was not on Earth. The footprint may last for a million years or longer. That is because there is no air on the moon and no winds to blow the dust around.

The astronauts could jump much higher on the moon than on Earth. People weigh much less on the moon than they do on Earth. The moon's gravity is one-sixth that of Earth's. Gravity causes objects to have weight. In places where there is less gravity, you weigh less and you can jump higher. That's why the astronauts could leap about on the moon's surface. To find out what you would weigh on the moon, divide your weight by six.

The astronauts discovered that the moon is a silent, strange place. The moon has no air. Air carries sound. With no air, the moon is completely silent. Even when the astronauts broke rocks or used the rockets on their spaceship, sound could not be heard.

The sky on the moon is always black. On Earth, we can see stars only at night. On the moon, stars shine all the time.

The moon does not have air, water, clouds, rain, or snow. It does not have weather. But the surface of the moon does warm up or cool off. The ground gets very hot or very cold because there is no air to spread the heat. The temperatures in the daytime can be above the boiling point of water. At night, the temperature can drop hundreds of degrees below zero. The astronauts' space suits kept their bodies at the right temperature. The astronauts carried tanks on their backs which contained the air they needed for breathing.

Without air and water the moon's surface has not worn away very much. The surface has changed so little that it holds clues to the early history of the moon. The astronauts searched for these clues. They collected rocks and brought them back to Earth for study by scientists. They drilled holes in the moon to look beneath the surface. They set up instruments to find moonquakes and to learn about other conditions on the moon. They photographed whatever they saw.

Each Apollo crew brought back more information about the moon. This photograph of the moon's surface was taken by the crew of Apollo 15. The astronauts of Apollo 15 stayed nearly sixty-seven hours on the moon. They returned with 173 pounds of moon rocks and soil. Scientists all over the world studied the information the astronauts brought back. They learned that the moon is about the same age as Earth. But the moon's soil and rocks are different from Earth's. For instance, moon rocks contain no water at all, while almost all rocks on Earth contain a small amount of water.

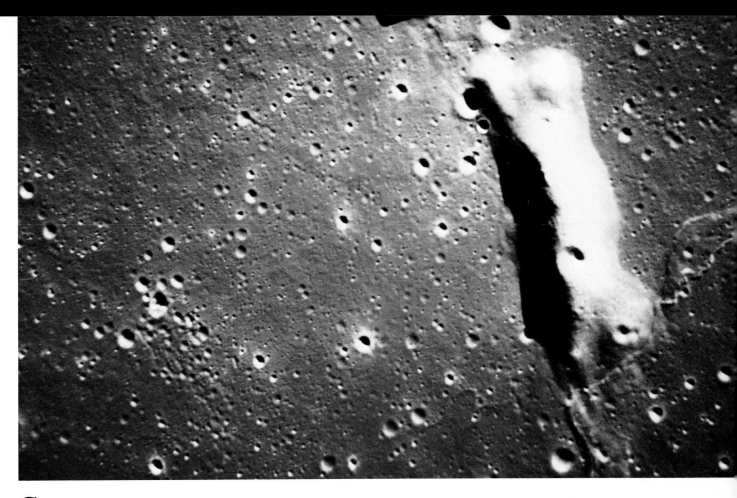

Scientists also learned that many millions of years ago, the inside of the moon was hot enough to melt rock. Melted rock, or lava, spilled over the surface of the moon. The lava formed lakes and then hardened. The solid lava became dark, black flat lands. This is a photograph of one of the flat lands on the moon. All of the small pits were made by rocks from space that hit the flat lands after they had hardened.

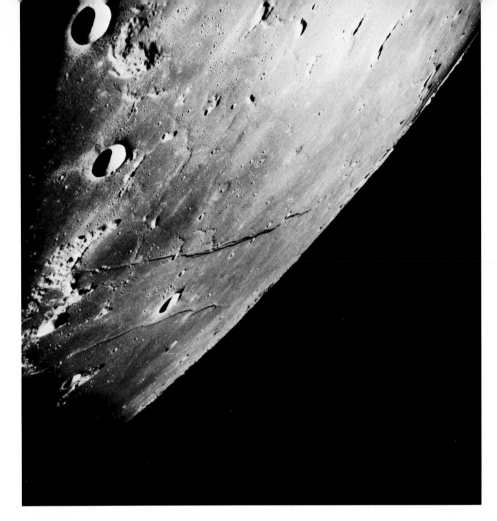

After millions of years, the inside of the moon cooled off. The lava stopped flowing. The moon then looked much as it does today. Its surface is covered with craters, mountains, valleys, and flat lands. There are very few changes on the moon today, but there are thousands of tiny moonquakes each year.

This is a photograph of a giant crater that is about fifty miles wide. The crater is named Tycho after a famous astronomer. The crater was formed when a huge rock from space crashed into the moon and buried itself. The rocks on the surface of the moon exploded. You can see the mountain peak that was formed in the center of the crater. The explosion also created the crater walls. Rocks and dust scattered for miles in all directions.

Apollo 17 was the last spaceship to carry people to the moon. It was launched in December, 1972. The astronauts of Apollo 17 discovered the oldest rock ever found on the moon. Scientists on Earth tested the rock. They discovered that it was more than 4,500 million years old. They named it the Genesis rock. Before the astronauts returned to Earth, they left a plaque on the moon showing the history of moon travel. They also left a falcon feather and a four-leaf clover. The feather and the four-leaf clover stand for the living things of Earth.

Scientists have learned much about the moon from the Apollo space flights. They have found the answers to many questions they once had. But in science, the answer to one question often raises a new question. For example, the flights around the moon showed what the far side of the moon looks like. But now scientists wonder why the far side of the moon has fewer flat lands than the near side. Much about the moon still remains a mystery.

Earth and its moon are close in space, but very different from each other. Earth is a blue, cloud-covered planet, filled with living things. The moon is a dead world. Without air or water, a cloud can never appear in its black sky and a raindrop will never fall.

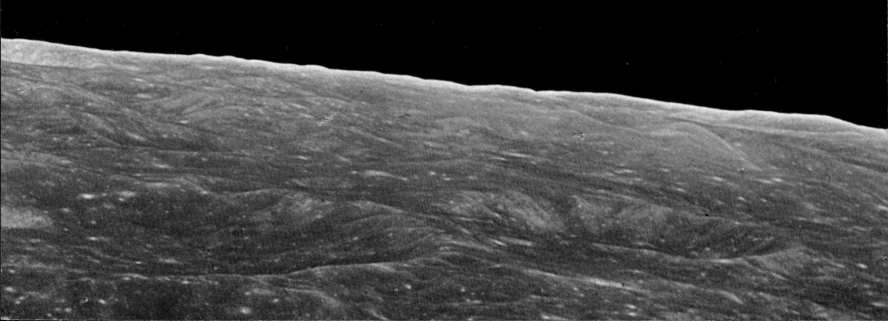

ACKNOWLEDGMENTS

FROM JENNY RISHER:

Courtney Smith, for your patience, love, friendship, and willingness to go on my crazy adventures. I dedicate my work to you. **Alexander** and **Oliver Smith,** for filling my days with happiness and joy. **Nancy Risher,** for loving and encouraging me through whatever ambitions I may have. **William Risher,** for instilling the photo bug in me. **Elizabeth Rhodes,** for being there on a moment's notice. **Matt Lee,** for seeing this through. We did it! **Ralph Menneneyer,** for your infectious enthusiasm. **Dan Staroff,** for pushing every pixel in these portraits to perfection with your talented eye. **Veronica Webb,** for inspiring me with the original idea. **Daniel Martin,** for connecting the dots. **Kathy Moore,** for your wisdom and guidance. **Patricia Willoughby, Roger Bunton,** and **Carlos Diaz,** for putting it into focus. **Timothy White,** for your encouragement. **John Varvatos,** for being the first. **John Balardo, Ed Peabody, Rebecca Powers, Steve Wilke,** and **Cassidy Zobl,** for your support. **Shirley Washington,** for your kindness. **Gregg Sutter,** for inspiring the name of this book—*Heart Soul Detroit.*

FROM MATT LEE:

Thank you to **Mama Lee, Brother Chris, Grandma Humphries, Lady Rebecca, George** and **Melba Dodson,** the **Saelzler-Sinclair Clan** and two friends and mentors whose writing advice I have (nearly) always taken, **George Bulanda** and **Joseph Epstein.** And, of course, an enormous thank you to the phenomenally talented and visionary **Jenny Risher** for bringing me on board with this amazing project.

Most important of all are the following people, who gave so freely of their time, trust, and so generously shared their stories of Detroit with us. Without them, this book would not have been possible:

Mitch Albom, Tim Allen, Juan Atkins, Selma Blair, Bill Bonds, Jerry Bruckheimer, George Clinton, Congressman John Conyers Jr., Alice Cooper, Eminem, Mel Farr, Bill Ford Jr., Sutton Foster, Berry Gordy, Tyree Guyton, Chris Hansen, Thomas Hearns, James P. Hoffa, Holland-Dozier-Holland, Willie Horton, Lee Iacocca, Al Kaline, Jackie Kallen, Dr. Jack Kevorkian, Wayne Kramer, Elmore Leonard, Senator Carl Levin, Philip Levine, Nicklas Lidström, Syd Mead, Ted Nugent, Iggy Pop, Dick Purtan, Della Reese, Martha Reeves, Claudette Robinson, Shaun Robinson, Smokey Robinson, Mitch Ryder, Barry Sanders, John Sinclair, Emanuel Steward, Anna Sui, Lily Tomlin, James Toney, John Varvatos, Don Was, Veronica Webb, Jack White, Allee Willis, and Mary Wilson.

In addition, this book could not have been completed without the following:

Lily Alt, Gina Alyse Lengyel, Leslie Ann Pilling, Shawn Armiak, Bob Babbit, Brent Bacher, Jeanine Barone, Johnnie Bassett, Saisha Beechman, Marcus Belgrave, Joan Belgrave, JB Bernstein, Karen Bonds, Art Bonus, Earl Bryant, Regina Carter, Scott Cassettari, Billie Causieestko, Lindsay Chase, Paul Cilione, Jeff Coleman, Valerie Laven-Cooper, Jim Crawford, DaVonne Darby, Mark Dehem, Melanie Demarco, Tyler Demogenes, Dennis Dennehy, Barbara Dozier, Mikey Eckstein, Jason Engstrom, Doug Ewing, Donna Faircloth, Duke Fakir, Michelle Figurski, Beth Franco, Joann Gambino (Siren Studios), Katie Heit Gardner, Gena Gatewood, Christine Gatti, Frances Glandney, Mayer Hawthorne, Elgene Hernandez, Ruth Holmes, Hilmer Kenty, Life Knyper, Harry Kong, Margaret Saadi Kramer, Robert Kreipke, Susan Krusel, Dan Kuzmarov, Andre LaRoche (Stage 3), Paul Lambert, Andrew Leff, Nansci Neiman LeGette, Yolonda Lipsey, Mark Macedo, Toby Mamis, Kristina Marra, Daniel Martin, Robert Matheu, Laura Matula, Roderick McClary, Milton McCrory, Henry McGroggan, Linda McIntosh, Rob McIntosh, Marisa Menzel, Joe Messina, Ruben Natal-San Miguel, Thomas Miller, Michael John Moore, Melanie T. Morgan, Mayer Morganroth, Janice Mowery, Troy Nankin, Niagara, Gjysta Nuculaj, Toby Nugent, George Ortiz, Paradime, Camilo Pardo, Stuart Parr, Ken Paves, Freda Payne, Jackson Perry, Linda Peterson, Dave Polzin, Maxine Powell, Tracy Reese, Jesus Roalandini, Bobby Rogers, Joan Hughes Rogers, Paul Rosenberg, Marc 'Rosey' Rosenthal, Anita Ruiz, Justin Ruppel, Norma Saken, Jackie Sanchez, Dontay Savoy, Carlon Scott, Roger Servick, Lois Shaevsky, Kim Silarski, Brad Simmons, Michael Singer, Amanda Sosa-Stone, Tiffany Steffens, Dee Suber, Elizabeth Sullivan, Kimberly Tauber, Brad Thomas, Peggy Thompson, Beverly Todd, Trick Trick, Steven Unger, Chris Voss, Spencer Weisberg, Jill Weiss, Angie Wells, Jenenne Whitfield, Marlene Williams, Eddie Willis, Cassandra Woods, and James Wrona.

Photographer: Jenny Risher
Writer, Editor: Matt Lee
Retoucher: Dan Staroff Studios
Book Design: Peter DiBartolo, Saturday LLC
Book Production: Aloli Press
Transcriber: Sandi White
Proofreader: Marie Look
Momentum Books: Ed Peabody

A portion of the proceeds from book sales will go to Focus: HOPE
focushope.edu

Heart Soul Detroit
heartsouldetroit.com

MOMENTUM BOOKS
First published in 2013 by: Momentum Books
momentumbooks.com

LCCN: 2012952764
ISBN: 978-1-938018-00-8
Printed in Singapore
First Printing, 2013